INLINE SKATING

BY JOHN HAMILTON

A&D Xtreme
An imprint of Abdo Publishing | www.abdopublishing.com

Visit us at
www.abdopublishing.com

Published by Abdo Publishing Company, a division of ABDO, PO Box 398166, Minneapolis, Minnesota 55439. Copyright ©2015 by Abdo Consulting Group, Inc. International copyrights reserved in all countries. No part of this book may be reproduced in any form without written permission from the publisher. A&D Xtreme™ is a trademark and logo of Abdo Publishing Company.

Printed in the United States of America, North Mankato, Minnesota.
052014
092014

PRINTED ON RECYCLED PAPER

Editor: Sue Hamilton
Graphic Design: Sue Hamilton
Cover Design: John Hamilton
Cover Photo: Corbis
Interior Photos: AP-pg 7; Corbis-pgs 4-5, 12-13, 15, 18, 19, 22-23, 24-25 & 26-27; Getty Images-pgs 14 & 20; Glow Images-pgs 1, 17 & 21; Koen Miseur-pgs 28-29; Rollerblade® USA-pgs 8, 10, 11, 16 (top) & 17; Science Source-pg 9; Scott Olson-pg 6; Thinkstock-pgs 2-3, 13 (inset); 16 (bottom), 30-31 & 32.

Websites
To learn more about Action Sports, visit booklinks.abdopublishing.com.
These links are routinely monitored and updated to provide the most current information available.

Library of Congress Control Number: 2014932222

Cataloging-in-Publication Data

Hamilton, John.
 Inline skating / John Hamilton.
   p. cm. -- (Action sports)
Includes index.
ISBN 978-1-62403-441-1
1. In-line skating--Juvenile literature.   I. Title.
796.21--dc23

                                    2014932222

CONTENTS

Inline Skating. 4

History. 6

Skates 8

Safety Gear 10

Aggressive Street 12

Aggressive Park 14

Vert 18

Freestyle Slalom. 20

Speed Skating 22

Downhill. 24

Hockey. 26

Inline World Championship 28

Glossary. 30

Index 32

INLINE SKATING

From streets and skateparks to hand railings, ramps, and even chains, inline skaters strap on wheeled boots and roll on. Balance and daring help inline skaters create wild moves on the narrowest of surfaces. They also whip down paths, streets, and mountains at crazy speeds. Control is rule number one.

Xtreme Fact: Inline skating is also known as rollerblading, blading, skating, or rolling.

HISTORY

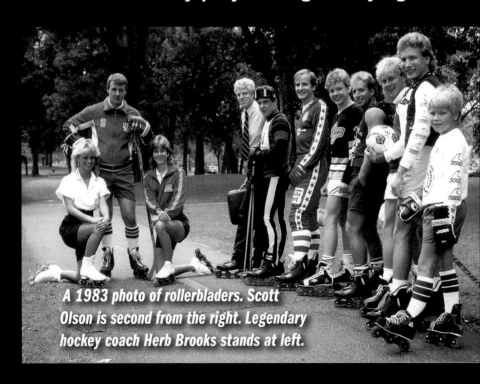

Early Hockey Rollerblades

Modern inline skating began when Minnesota brothers Scott and Brennan Olson put skateboard wheels on roller skate boots in 1980. By lining up all the wheels, they could practice their hockey moves on paved roads in the summer. The Olsons patented the skate design and called their creation Rollerblades. Skiers and hockey players began buying them.

A 1983 photo of rollerbladers. Scott Olson is second from the right. Legendary hockey coach Herb Brooks stands at left.

6

Inline skates looked fun, and soon roller skaters wanted them as well. Since Rollerblade was the only company producing these skates, the term "rollerblading" became popular. Inline skating is still often called rollerblading, although several companies now make their own brands of inline skates.

Xtreme Fact: John Joseph Merlin of Belgium invented the first inline skates in 1760. He never figured out how to stop while wearing them, so he never patented his design. He is known as the father of inline skating.

SKATES

Inline skates have a boot with tough wheels, which are usually made of polyurethane. The skates are often designed with a heel brake. The wheels vary in size and hardness, depending on what the wearer wants to do. Smaller wheels equal better balance. Softer wheels give better traction and cornering. Hard wheels result in faster speeds on smooth surfaces.

PARTS OF AN INLINE SKATE

Pull Strap

Buckle

Boot Cuff

Cuff Bolt

Heel Brake

Boot

Laces

Air Vent

Frame

Wheel

Brake Pad

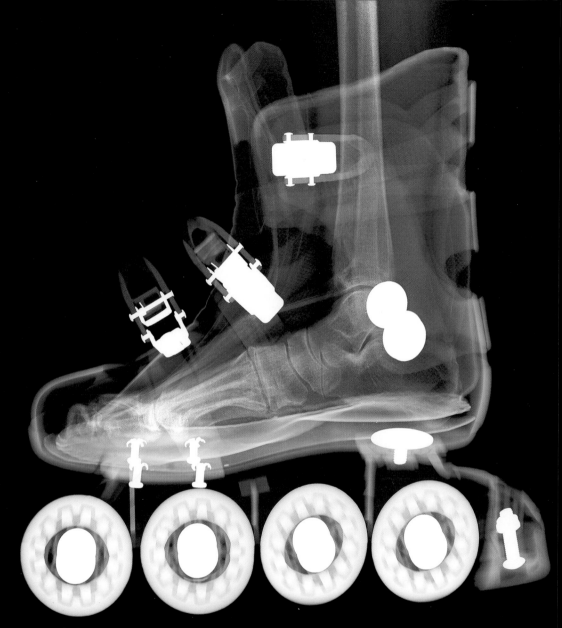

Although most inline skates have four wheels, some smaller-sized skates have just three. Speed or race skates often have five narrow wheels. This allows for more stability with the least amount of road friction.

SAFETY GEAR

To protect themselves, inline skaters wear what they call "armor." The most important piece is a helmet. Helmets are made of styrofoam with a laminated shell. They are lightweight to prevent neck strain. Helmets fit snuggly, which helps protect the brain from being jostled around during a collision.

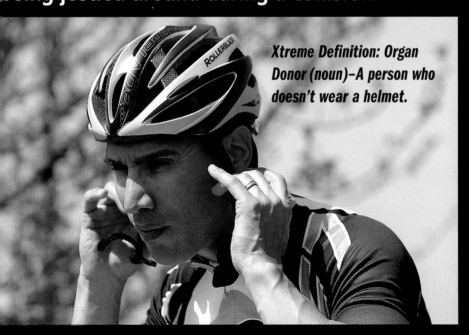

Xtreme Definition: Organ Donor (noun)–A person who doesn't wear a helmet.

Inline skaters also wear gloves and wrist guards. They protect the palms when falling, as well as help prevent wrist injuries. Knee and elbow pads, or "sliders," also protect skaters during a fall.

11

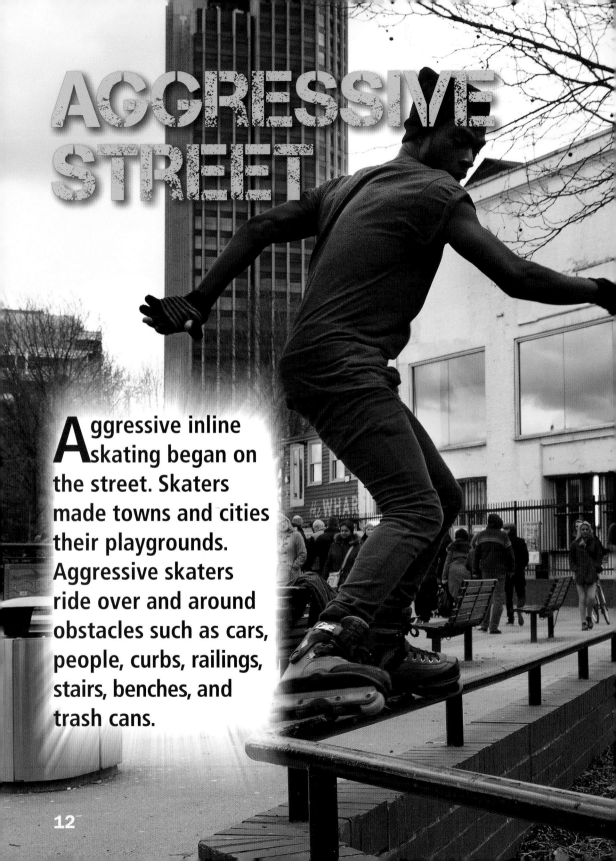

AGGRESSIVE STREET

Aggressive inline skating began on the street. Skaters made towns and cities their playgrounds. Aggressive skaters ride over and around obstacles such as cars, people, curbs, railings, stairs, benches, and trash cans.

Xtreme Fact: After some dangerous, out-of-control skating, some cities posted signs making inline skating illegal around heavily populated areas.

AGGRESSIVE PARK

An inline skater performs on a wooden half-pipe.

Aggressive inline allows skaters to perform aerial tricks from a ramp. Many skateparks include quarter-pipes, half-pipes, and bowls. A series of tricks is known as a "line."

Chris Haffey performs an inline skate routine in 2013.

Aggressive skaters perform such tricks as railing, grinds, stalls, spins, and slides.

Patrick Francisco performs a trick in a skatepark bowl.

An inline skater on a free-standing grind rail.

Jeremy Suarez performs a trick on the coping.

VERT

Vert skating refers to vertical moves on inline skates. Skaters drop in and pick up speed on 8- and 12-foot (2.4- and 3.7-m) -high wood or concrete ramps. As they accelerate, they move up and beyond the attached curved wall to "catch air." Of course, knowing how to land is vitally important to a vert skater's health. Vert skaters perform flips, spins, rotations, grabs, and lip tricks.

Jaren Grob competes in ESPN's men's vert half-pipe in Georgia in 2002.

Xtreme Fact: Fabiola da Silva became the first woman to pull a double back flip on a vert ramp during a 2005 competition. Only a few pro skaters have successfully completed this trick.

Fabiola da Silva of São Paulo, Brazil, competes in an inline vert competition during the 2003 Gravity Games.

FREESTYLE SLALOM

Freestyle slalom skaters compete on flat surfaces. Skaters perform balance, control, and technical tricks around narrowly-spaced cones. Top freestyle slalom tricks include crisscrosses, snakes, eagles, and footguns.

Xtreme Fact: Freestyle slalom is also known as cone skating.

21

SPEED SKATING

Inline speed skating is furiously fast racing. Skaters wear 4- or 5-wheeled, low-cut skates. Some racers compete on 100-meter (328-ft) indoor oval tracks. Other speed skating races take place outside on closed-to-traffic loops or sections of roads.

Xtreme Fact: Inline speed skaters have been recorded going 68 miles per hour (109 kph). The average speed skater goes about 15 mph (24 kph).

Speed skating races are sprints that range from 100 meters (328 feet) to 5 kilometers (3.1 miles). Marathons take racers cross-country. A common marathon distance is 26.2 miles (42 km).

Colombian speed skater Liana Holguin competes during the 2006 Odesur South American Games in Mar del Plata, Argentina.

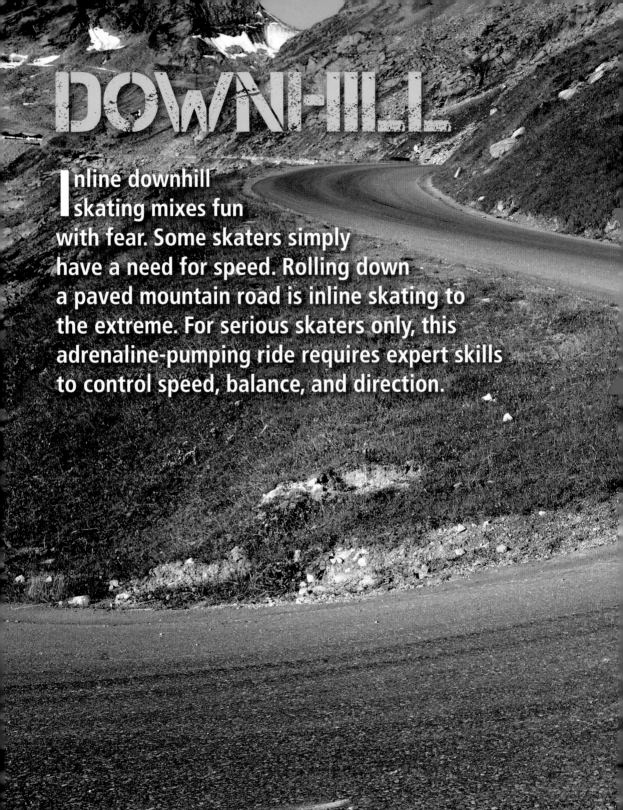

DOWNHILL

Inline downhill
skating mixes fun
with fear. Some skaters simply
have a need for speed. Rolling down
a paved mountain road is inline skating to
the extreme. For serious skaters only, this
adrenaline-pumping ride requires expert skills
to control speed, balance, and direction.

Whether racing against the clock or other skaters, danger always lurks around the next hairpin curve. Essential gear includes special pads, protective suits, and aerodynamic helmets. Downhill inline skates have long frames and soft urethane wheels. Many are custom built.

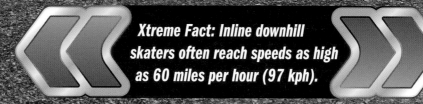

Xtreme Fact: Inline downhill skaters often reach speeds as high as 60 miles per hour (97 kph).

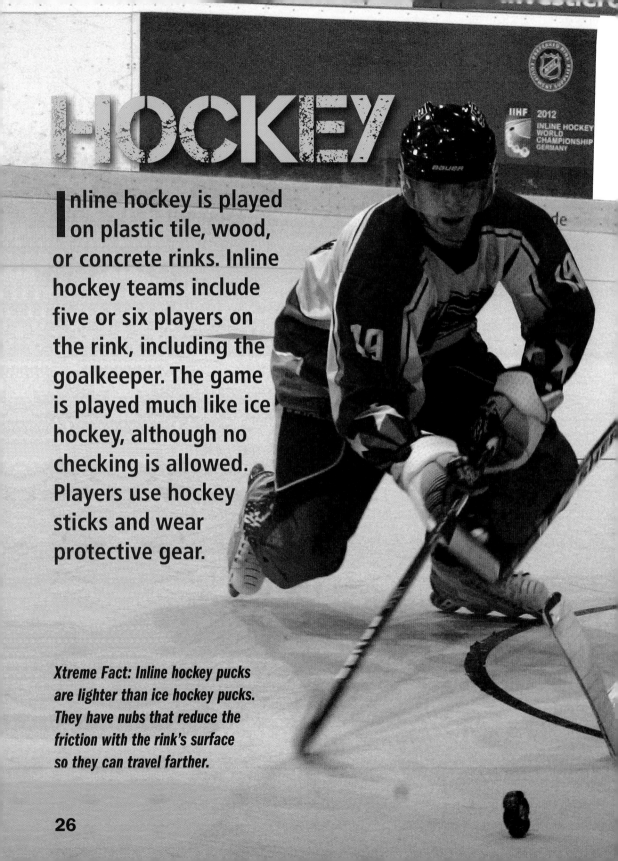

HOCKEY

IIHF 2012 INLINE HOCKEY WORLD CHAMPIONSHIP GERMANY

Inline hockey is played on plastic tile, wood, or concrete rinks. Inline hockey teams include five or six players on the rink, including the goalkeeper. The game is played much like ice hockey, although no checking is allowed. Players use hockey sticks and wear protective gear.

Xtreme Fact: Inline hockey pucks are lighter than ice hockey pucks. They have nubs that reduce the friction with the rink's surface so they can travel farther.

The United States plays Canada during the Inline Hockey World Championship in 2012.

INLINE WORLD CHAMPIONSHIP

The best inline skaters compete in the Inline World Championship. It is organized by FIRS (Federation Internationale de Roller Sports). It was last held in Oostende, Belgium, in 2013. Competitive events include sprints, relays, speed skating, and marathons.

GLOSSARY

Accelerate
The increasing speed of an object, such as a skater going from a standstill to 15 miles per hour (24 kph) in a short period of time.

Adrenaline
A chemical created in the human body that is released when a person feels strong emotions such as fear or excitement. Adrenaline causes the heart to beat faster and gives a person quick energy.

Aerodynamic
Something that has a shape that reduces the drag, or resistance, of air moving across its surface. Helmets with aerodynamic shapes help racers go faster because they don't have to push as hard to get through the air.

Bowl
A wooden or cement bowl-shaped skating surface that is built in skateparks. The idea arose from skaters practicing in empty pools. Bowls are usually 3 to 12 feet (.9 to 3.7 m) deep.

Coping

A narrow, usually metal pipe at the top edge of ramps.

ESPN

A television network that broadcasts entertainment and sports programming.

Grinds

To slide across an obstacle such as a curb or railing without rolling on the wheels of the skate.

Half-Pipe

A large, U-shaped ramp used to perform jumps and tricks by such athletes as inline skaters.

Quarter-Pipe

A ramp that is half the size of a half-pipe. It is used to perform jumps and tricks.

Rail

A metal surface, such as a handrailing, that a skater jumps on and slides down its length.

Stall

A trick where the skater rolls up and stops moving briefly, or "stalls."

INDEX

A
aerial tricks 14
aggressive inline
   skating 12, 14
Argentina 23
armor 10

B
Belgium 7,
   28
bowl 14, 16
Brazil 19

C
Canada 27
cone skating 21
coping 17

D
da Silva, Fabiola 19
downhill inline skating
   24, 25

E
ESPN 18

F
FIRS (Federation
   Internationale de
   Roller Sports) 28
Francisco, Patrick 16
freestyle slalom skating
   20, 21

G
Georgia 18
Gravity Games 19
Grob, Jaren 18

H
Haffey, Chris 15
half-pipe 14, 18
hockey, inline 26
Holguin, Liana 23

I
Inline Hockey World
   Championship 27
Inline World
   Championship 28

L
line 14

M
Mar del Plata, Argentina
   23
Merlin, John Joseph 7
Minnesota 6

O
Odesur South American
   Games 23
Olson, Brennan 6
Olson, Scott 6
Oostende, Belgium 28

Q
quarter-pipe 14

R
rail 16
ramp 4, 14, 18, 19
Rollerblade 6, 7

S
São Paulo, Brazil 19
sliders 11
speed skating, inline
   22, 23
Suarez, Jeremy 17

U
United States 27

V
vert inline skating 18,
   19